THE OFFICIAL SOUTHAMPTON FOOTBALL CLUB ANNUAL 2020

WRITTEN BY MARK PERROW
DESIGNED BY JON DALRYMPLE

A Grange Publication

ISBN 978-1-913034-30-6

CONTENTS

WELCOME

TO THE OFFICIAL SOUTHAMPTON FOOTBALL CLUB ANNUAL 2020!

It's packed full of fun features for Saints fanatics of all ages to get stuck into!

We start with a look back on 2018/19 – a season in which Saints experienced contrasting fortunes before and after the appointment of charismatic manager Ralph Hasenhüttl.

Ultimately, we're celebrating another year of Premier League football at St Mary's, and here you can remember all the highs and lows along the way, including the best goals, assists, saves and matches of Saints' seventh successive top-flight campaign.

We pay tribute to record-breaking Saint Shane Long, who made history with his early strike at Watford in April, and ask Angus Gunn for his penalty-saving tips after Saints' last line of defence kept out Theo Walcott and Paul Pogba from the spot.

We're also looking back on an eventful decade for the club that began in League One and included back-to-back promotions en route to the return of European football at St Mary's.

Test your knowledge on all things Saints with our unique collection of quizzes and games, and check out all the best behind-the scenes photos from another roller-coaster campaign!

Enjoy your read!

AUGUST

Saints would have to wait an extra day to kick off their 2018/19 campaign, with first opponents Burnley already in the swing of competitive action in the Europa League.

Typically well-drilled and resilient, the visitors dug deep to earn a goalless draw, as even ex-Clarets striker and Saints debutant Danny Ings was unable to force a breakthrough.

The summer signing did open his account for his new club on Merseyside, albeit in a losing cause, as Goodison Park remained an unhappy hunting ground in a 2-1 defeat.

Saints signed off the month by progressing in the Carabao Cup courtesy of Charlie Austin's late header at Brighton, but had already been on the receiving end of a last-gasp winner themselves, as England World Cup hero Harry Maguire's low shot earned Leicester the points at St Mary's.

MOMENT OF THE MONTH ▶

Signed from Liverpool, Danny Ings was not the most popular goalscorer as he got off the mark at Everton.

PLAYER OF THE MONTH
RYAN BERTRAND
In a testing opening month for Saints, skipper Bertrand maintained his consistency and struck a brilliant equaliser from outside the box to bring St Mary's to life against Leicester.

RESULTS

Saints	0-0	Burnley	D
Everton	2-1	Saints	L
Saints	1-2	Leicester	L
Brighton	0-1	Saints	W Carabao Cup R2

SEPTEMBER

Determined to build on the cup success at Brighton, Saints secured back-to-back wins to get off the mark in the Premier League with a morale-boosting 2-0 victory at Crystal Palace.

Goalscorers Danny Ings and Pierre-Emile Højbjerg were on target again when Saints looked set to register another win over Brighton, only for the Seagulls to stage a late revival and salvage a point, as St Mary's witnessed another decisive stoppage-time strike in favour of the visiting team.

A daunting trip to early season pacesetters Liverpool saw Saints well beaten, 3-0 at Anfield, but a first visit to Molineux in nine years resulted in a more competitive contest.

Mark Hughes's men were well in the game until the closing stages, but two goals in the final 11 minutes condemned Saints to successive defeats.

MOMENT OF THE MONTH ▶

Pierre-Emile Højbjerg's crisp 30-yard strike flew into the bottom corner to give Saints the lead against Brighton.

PLAYER OF THE MONTH
DANNY INGS

Saints had struggled for goals in 2017/18 but finally had a striker brimming with confidence, as Ings found the net in successive matches to take his tally to three goals in four games.

RESULTS

Crystal Palace	0-2	Saints	W
Saints	2-2	Brighton	D
Liverpool	3-0	Saints	L
Wolves	2-0	Saints	L

OCTOBER

Surrendering a two-goal lead against Brighton would prove the start of a slippery slope for Saints, who would not win again in the league until December.

Respite arrived in the Carabao Cup, where Saints followed up their win at the Amex Stadium by ending a 21-year hoodoo at Goodison Park, inspired by Angus Gunn's penalty shoot-out heroics after Danny Ings had scored in open play.

Mark Hughes declared his team "too passive" as Chelsea ran out 3-0 winners at St Mary's, but ensured his side were tighter defensively in keeping back-to-back clean sheets against Bournemouth and Newcastle.

Only the finishing touch was missing, as Manolo Gabbiadini headed over late on at the Vitality Stadium, before 22 attempts at goal went unconverted against the Magpies.

MOMENT OF THE MONTH ▶

Angus Gunn's penalty save from ex-Saint Theo Walcott secured victory at Everton for the first time since 1997.

PLAYER OF THE MONTH
JACK STEPHENS
Restored to Mark Hughes's starting line-up after the home defeat to Chelsea, Stephens was a steadying influence in defence as he helped Saints to back-to-back Premier League clean sheets.

RESULTS

Everton	1-1	Saints*	D	*Carabao Cup R3*
Saints	0-3	Chelsea	L	
Bournemouth	0-0	Saints	D	
Saints	0-0	Newcastle	D	

*Saints won 4-3 on penalties

NOVEMBER

Just as Saints looked to have made themselves harder to break down, a date with Manchester City provided a stern reality check.

The champions would make a habit of racking up big scores, finding the net a staggering 169 times in all competitions, including six past Saints at the Etihad.

Manolo Gabbiadini broke the deadlock as Saints looked set to respond with a home victory over Watford, but the league's surprise package fought back to earn a share of the spoils.

A six-pointer followed at Fulham, where Stuart Armstrong scored his first two Premier League goals, but Claudio Ranieri celebrated a 3-2 win in his first match in charge of the struggling Londoners, before Saints exited the Carabao Cup on penalties after a goalless draw at Leicester.

MOMENT OF THE MONTH ▶

Having opened the scoring at Craven Cottage, Stuart Armstrong's precise curling shot levelled the scores at 2-2.

**PLAYER OF THE MONTH
STUART ARMSTRONG**
In a month with little to cheer, Armstrong's contribution at Fulham offered a glimpse of the Scot's obvious talent and ability to score goals from midfield.

RESULTS

Man City	6-1	Saints	L
Saints	1-1	Watford	D
Fulham	3-2	Saints	L
Leicester	0-0	Saints*	D *Carabao Cup R4*

*Saints lost 6-5 on penalties

DECEMBER

The Christmas period tends to be hectic at the best of times, but Saints' players were working overtime after the appointment of Ralph Hasenhüttl as the club's new manager.

Mark Hughes's final game at the helm was a 2-2 draw with Manchester United in which Saints let a two-goal lead slip, before Kelvin Davis stepped in for a 3-1 defeat at Tottenham.

Hasenhüttl's impact was not quite instant, as his side shot themselves in the foot at Cardiff, but his influence was clear as Saints played with greater intensity to shock an Arsenal team, who were 22 games unbeaten, 3-2 at St Mary's.

The feel-good factor was back and Saints scored three times again, at Huddersfield, securing successive league wins for the first time since April 2017, but home defeats to Manchester City and West Ham reminded the boss of the size of the task ahead.

MOMENT OF THE MONTH ▶

Charlie Austin's late header against Arsenal sent St Mary's into raptures, securing Ralph Hasenhüttl's first win in charge.

PLAYER OF THE MONTH
NATHAN REDMOND

Redmond felt he had been inching back to form, but was still waiting for his statistics to back that up, before finishing December with two goals, two assists and his confidence restored.

RESULTS

Saints	2-2	Man Utd	D
Tottenham	3-1	Saints	L
Cardiff	1-0	Saints	L
Saints	3-2	Arsenal	W
Huddersfield	1-3	Saints	W
Saints	1-2	West Ham	L
Saints	1-3	Man City	L

JANUARY

Saints' early progress under the new boss continued with an unbeaten start to 2019.

Angus Gunn celebrated his Premier League debut with a man-of-the-match display to keep a clean sheet at Chelsea, before Alex McCarthy was reinstated for crucial back-to-back league wins over Leicester and Everton.

Ralph Hasenhüttl's willingness to give youth a chance saw Callum Slattery and Marcus Barnes make their debuts away at Derby in the FA Cup, while Kayne Ramsay and Tyreke Johnson started the replay as both games finished 2-2, before Saints' fate was sealed on another penalty shoot-out.

The month finished with another draw, 1-1 with Crystal Palace, as James Ward-Prowse scored in a third consecutive Premier League match for the first time in his career.

MOMENT OF THE MONTH ▶

Shane Long celebrated his first goal of the season as ten-man Saints dug deep for a crucial win at Leicester.

PLAYER OF THE MONTH
JAMES WARD-PROWSE
Rejuvenated under Ralph Hasenhüttl's tutelage, Ward-Prowse's form earned the midfielder a Premier League Player of the Month nomination as he scored in three league games in a row.

RESULTS

Chelsea	0-0	Saints	D	
Derby	2-2	Saints	D	FA Cup R3
Leicester	1-2	Saints	W	
Saints	2-2	Derby	D	FA Cup R3 replay
Saints	2-1	Everton	W	
Saints	1-1	Crystal Palace	D	

*Saints lost 5-3 on penalties

FEBRUARY

Confidence restored, Saints eyed some attractive February fixtures as an opportunity to pull clear of trouble, but Nathan Redmond's fine solo goal at Burnley was cancelled out by a last-gasp penalty that rescued the hosts a point.

A home victory over Cardiff would have propelled Ralph Hasenhüttl's side five points clear of the drop zone, but instead they were back in it when the Bluebirds responded to Jack Stephens's late leveller with a stoppage-time winner of their own.

The trip to Arsenal always looked an uphill task, but Saints made it impossible by conceding two early goals at the Emirates.

The pressure was on when Fulham visited St Mary's, but goals from Oriol Romeu and James Ward-Prowse lifted Saints out of the bottom three to effectively end the Londoners' own survival hopes.

MOMENT OF THE MONTH ▶

Oriol Romeu's first goal in 15 months sent Saints on their way to victory on a pivotal night against Fulham.

PLAYER OF THE MONTH
JAN BEDNAREK
Another man with a new lease of life under the Ralph Hasenhüttl regime, Bednarek was back in from the cold and flourishing as a regular starter in an improving Saints defence.

RESULTS

Burnley	1-1	Saints	D
Saints	1-2	Cardiff	L
Arsenal	2-0	Saints	L
Saints	2-0	Fulham	W

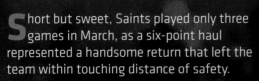

Short but sweet, Saints played only three games in March, as a six-point haul represented a handsome return that left the team within touching distance of safety.

Heading to Old Trafford to face a rejuvenated Manchester United may have been a daunting task for Ralph's rookies, but Yan Valery embodied the fearlessness of youth with a stunning strike to fire the underdogs in front.

United fought back to win a topsy-turvy game even after James Ward-Prowse's brilliant free-kick, but Saints were proving they could mix it with the best, and the same pair were on target to overturn a half-time deficit and stun Tottenham at St Mary's.

Next up was a survival six-pointer at Brighton, where Saints ran out deserving winners thanks to Pierre-Emile Højbjerg's decisive strike early in the second half.

MOMENT OF THE MONTH ▶

James Ward-Prowse followed up his set-piece heroics at Old Trafford with another superb free-kick to see off Spurs.

PLAYER OF THE MONTH
YAN VALERY

After Cédric's January departure to Inter Milan, Valery excelled on the right flank, scoring his first two goals in successive games against two Champions League quarter-finalists.

RESULTS

Man Utd	3-2	Saints	L
Saints	2-1	Tottenham	W
Brighton	0-1	Saints	W

APRIL

With Liverpool gunning for the title, Saints were quick out of the blocks to give the Reds a fright, only to be undone by two late goals.

But a 3-1 victory over Wolves the following week, inspired by Nathan Redmond's first-half brace, left Saints within touching distance of survival.

Two quick-fire goals left Ralph Hasenhüttl's men with too much to do at Newcastle,

despite Mario Lemina scoring on his return from injury, but nobody has ever been faster out of the blocks than Shane Long at Watford, as the striker made history by finding the net in just 7.69 seconds – a new Premier League record.

The Hornets' late equaliser and results elsewhere left Saints needing one more point to be safe – cue a thrilling 3-3 draw against south coast neighbours Bournemouth, with Matt Targett's first goal for the club sparking scenes of relief as the final whistle sounded at St Mary's.

MOMENT OF THE MONTH ▶

Shane Long raced through on goal straight from kick-off to score at Watford and make Premier League history.

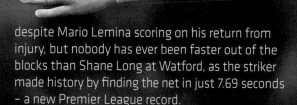

PLAYER OF THE MONTH
SHANE LONG
Long's record-breaking moment at Vicarage Road was one of four goals in April for the in-form striker, who also found the net in the home games against Liverpool, Wolves and Bournemouth.

RESULTS

Saints	1-3	Liverpool	L
Saints	3-1	Wolves	W
Newcastle	3-1	Saints	L
Watford	1-1	Saints	D
Saints	3-3	Bournemouth	D

MAY

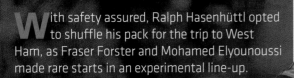

With safety assured, Ralph Hasenhüttl opted to shuffle his pack for the trip to West Ham, as Fraser Forster and Mohamed Elyounoussi made rare starts in an experimental line-up.

However, it was Hasenhüttl's Austrian compatriot Marko Arnautović who played an influential role, scoring either side of half time as the Hammers signed off in style in their last home game of the season.

To the final day, where victory over relegated Huddersfield would have taken Saints beyond the 40-point mark, which looked likely when Nathan Redmond crashed home a spectacular first-half opener.

But the Terriers would not lie down and Alex Pritchard profited from a rare lapse by Angus Gunn, leaving Saints having to settle for a point before bidding farewell to their supporters with a traditional lap of appreciation.

MOMENT OF THE MONTH ▶

In scoring Saints' last goal of the season, Nathan Redmond reached a career high of nine for the campaign.

PLAYER OF THE MONTH
PIERRE-EMILE HØJBJERG
In good times and bad, captain Højbjerg guarantees one hundred per cent effort every time he pulls on the shirt – even at a stage when survival was assured and results less critical.

RESULTS

West Ham	3-0	Saints	L
Saints	1-1	Huddersfield	D

FINAL PREMIER LEAGUE TABLE

		Pld	Pts	GD
1	Man City (C)	38	98	72
2	Liverpool	38	97	67
3	Chelsea	38	72	24
4	Tottenham	38	71	28
5	Arsenal	38	70	22
6	Man United	38	66	11
7	Wolves	38	57	1
8	Everton	38	54	8
9	Leicester	38	52	3
10	West Ham	38	52	-3
11	Watford	38	50	-7
12	Crystal Palace	38	49	-2
13	Newcastle	38	45	-6
14	Bournemouth	38	45	-14
15	Burnley	38	40	-23
16	SAINTS	38	39	-20
17	Brighton	38	36	-25
18	Cardiff (R)	38	34	-35
19	Fulham (R)	38	26	-47
20	Huddersfield (R)	38	16	-54

PLAYER AWARDS

Nathan Redmond took centre stage as Southampton's 2018/19 awards were handed out in a glittering ceremony at St Mary's, celebrating the achievements of the first team, Academy and women's teams, and the influential players along the way...

Virgin Media Fans' Player of the Season
NATHAN REDMOND

Winger Redmond was recognised by the Saints supporters for his impressive transformation in 2018/19, having lost confidence in himself – by his own admission – the previous season.

He started the campaign by restoring positivity and directness to his game, but it was the arrival of Ralph Hasenhüttl as manager in December that took him to new heights.

Under Armour Players' Player of the Season
NATHAN REDMOND

Completing the double, Redmond also earned the votes of his teammates, who recognised his commitment and dedication in returning to top form.

'The boys in the dressing room, the manager and the coaching staff have enabled me to play with confidence and affect games in a positive way" he revealed, upon receiving the award

Under Armour First-Team Young Player of the Year
VAN VALERY

Another man to pick up two prizes on the night, and another who shot to prominence in the second half of the campaign.

Making his senior debut in November, Valery made the position his own after Cédric's departure on loan to Inter Milan in January, emerging as one of the finds of the season.

Utilita Goal of the Season
YAN VALERY

Valery's smooth transition into the first team was most evident when he received the ball 40 yards from goal at Old Trafford with the game still goalless.

The Frenchman had never scored a goal in his senior career, but had the confidence to drive forward and send an explosive shot flying past David De Gea into the top corner

President's Choice Award
JAMES WARD-PROWSE

Every year, club president Terry Paine MBE picks out one player he believes made a standout contribution to the team and great strides in his own performance.

In 2018/19, James Ward-Prowse was that man, with the midfielder rewarded for adding steel and end product to his game, finishing the season with a career high seven Premier League goals.

Solent University Academy
Young Player of the Year
WILL FERRY

A promising left winger, the teenager has been a star performer for Saints' Under-18s, whilst also helping the Under-23s win promotion from Premier League 2 Division Two.

Ferry, signed from Bury in 2017, is also a Republic of Ireland youth international and will hope to continue progressing through the ranks at Staplewood.

Virgin Media Women's
Player of the Year
SHANNON SIEVWRIGHT

Sievwright was recognised as the outstanding player in an all-conquering season for Southampton FC Women, who secured the league and cup double.

"The main thing that's stood out for me is how much I've grown as a person as well as a player, because of my teammates pushing me every single day," she said of the accolade.

Solent University Girls' Regional
Talent Club Player of the Year
CAITLIN SMITH

Each year, a promising young female player is rewarded for their development, as Saints' Regional Talent Club continues to go from strength to strength.

The 2018/19 winner was Caitlin Smith, who follows in the footsteps of England youth international Kiera Skeels, now of Reading FC Women.

QUIZ OF T

1. How many first-team players did Saints sign in the 2018 summer transfer window?

2. Who was the only senior player to be sold before the start of the season?

3. Which club did Guido Carrillo join on a season-long loan?

4. Saints rallied from 2-0 down to win their penultimate pre-season friendly at St Mary's against which European club?

5. Who scored Saints' first home goal of the 2018/19 Premier League campaign?

6. Saints played in five cup ties in 2018/19. How many were at St Mary's?

7. Mark Hughes's only back-to-back wins in charge saw Saints defeat which two teams?

8. True or false? Hughes's last three home games as Saints boss were all drawn.

9. Who scored the club's first goal under Ralph Hasenhüttl?

10. Who made their senior debut as a late substitute that day?

11 Which two players enjoyed an early Christmas present by scoring their first goal of the season at Huddersfield?

12 Who was the only Saint to be sent off twice in 2018/19?

13 Who produced a man-of-the-match display on his Premier League debut in Saints' first match of 2019?

14 Saints waved goodbye to two popular players in January. Who were they?

15 How many penalty shoot-outs were Saints involved in throughout the season?

16 How many times did Saints win back-to-back league games under Hasenhüttl in 2018/19?

17 Who was the only Saint to be nominated for the Premier League Player of the Month award twice?

18 Who were the only team Shane Long did not score against in Saints' five April fixtures?

19 Who netted his first Saints goal on his penultimate appearance for the club?

20 How many Academy graduates made their first-team debuts in 2018/19, in all competitions?

15

18

Answers on page 60

TOP **5** GOALS

① YAN VALERY vs Man Utd (A)

Voted Saints' Goal of the Season, it's remarkable to think Valery had never scored at senior level when he received the ball from Charlie Austin, 40 yards from goal. Advancing into space, the Frenchman took a touch out of his feet and unleashed an unstoppable shot that flew past David De Gea to silence Old Trafford.

PIERRE-EMILE HØJBJERG vs Brighton (H)

As pure a strike as you could ever wish to see, Højbjerg cushioned a Brighton clearance into his path, surveyed the scene and opted to try his luck. Cutting across the ball with his instep, his 30-yard shot was going wide before it curled back just inside the far post, nestling beautifully into the bottom corner.

②

③ JAMES WARD-PROWSE vs Tottenham (H)

As crucial as it was spectacular, this trademark Ward-Prowse free-kick was his second in as many games. Following a brilliant strike at Old Trafford the week before, this time he was closer to goal with less room to dip it back down after clearing the wall, but World Cup winner Hugo Lloris was beaten all ends up.

STUART ARMSTRONG vs Fulham (A)

The game that announced Armstrong's arrival in the Premier League, the Scottish international had already opened his account to give Saints the lead, but it was his second that really stands out. Stepping on to Cédric's clever backheel, the midfielder dispatched an unerring first-time shot that flew into the top corner.

④

⑤ NATHAN REDMOND vs Huddersfield (H)

This was not the most memorable end-of-season affair, but Redmond did his bit to light up St Mary's with an electrifying opener. Slowing down his full-back, the winger dropped a shoulder and surged inside, taking a second touch away from the next man before whipping a fine curling shot just underneath the crossbar.

TOP **5** ASSISTS

1 MATT TARGETT vs Arsenal (H)

Perhaps the game of the season at St Mary's, and it was Targett who set Saints on their way to victory with a sublime cross. Receiving the ball wide on the left, the Academy graduate manufactured enough space to curl the ball around Héctor Bellerín with a delivery so good Danny Ings just had to apply the final touch.

SHANE LONG vs Arsenal (H)

With five minutes to go and the scores level, substitute Long set off on one of his willing runs into the channel as Saints launched a counter-attack. In need of support, the Irishman waited for his strike partner to arrive before clipping the ball up to the far post, just out of reach of Bernd Leno, for Charlie Austin to win the game.

3 CÉDRIC vs Fulham (A)

This was an enthralling end-to-end contest at Craven Cottage, which goes some way to explaining Cédric's position on the edge of the Fulham box. With little room to play with, the defender improvised with a cute backheel, knowing Stuart Armstrong was behind him, allowing the Scot to shoot first time with an unstoppable strike.

JACK STEPHENS vs Derby (H)

Jack Stephens can be a fine exponent of how to bring the ball out of defence, as demonstrated to deadly effect in this FA Cup third round replay. Receiving the ball midway inside his own half, he confidently shimmied away from Jack Marriott, strode into midfield and picked out Nathan Redmond with a defence-splitting pass.

5 YAN VALERY vs Bournemouth (H)

The goal that effectively secured Saints' Premier League survival saw one wing-back combine with the other. Valery needed all his pace and power to get the better of Bournemouth's star defender, Nathan Aké, before producing a cross begging to be attacked by Matt Targett, who gleefully headed home at the far post.

TOP **5** SAVES

① ANGUS GUNN vs Newcastle (A)

Quite brilliant reflexes from the young keeper, who looked beaten when Isaac Hayden's crisp volley took a significant deflection off Maya Yoshida. Gunn had already moved to his right, but somehow adjusted his body and stuck out a left hand to repel the shot, which was flying goalwards and seemingly destined for the net.

ALEX MCCARTHY vs Wolves (A)

② It looked for all the world that Saints were about to fall behind at Molineux, only for McCarthy to intervene. João Moutinho's cross was swinging in towards McCarthy's goal, and the keeper had little time to adjust when Raúl Jiménez helped it on with a glancing header, but a remarkable one-handed tip over kept the Mexican at bay.

③ ALEX MCCARTHY vs Man City (H)

Man City do not like to take potshots from anywhere, but when David Silva stepped away from Jack Stephens, the Spaniard had little choice – he was eight yards out with a free sight of goal. Many keepers would have given up, but McCarthy spread himself and somehow repelled Silva's effort with an outstretched left hand.

ANGUS GUNN vs Man Utd (A)

④ The sort of save that needs a replay to be fully appreciated, Gunn could only get fingertips to Romelu Lukaku's skidding shot, but that was enough to turn the ball aside. The Belgian striker hammered a low drive towards the bottom corner, where Saints' last line of defence found just enough strength to keep him out.

⑤ ANGUS GUNN vs Chelsea (A)

Perhaps the best goalkeeping performance of Saints' season, Gunn celebrated his Premier League debut with a clean sheet at Stamford Bridge. The pick of his six saves came in the first half, when Eden Hazard rifled a shot from close range, but the rookie keeper raised his hands just in time – above his head – to preserve parity.

TOP **5** MATCHES

SAINTS 3-2 ARSENAL

The day that welcomed a new dawn, Ralph Hasenhüttl showcased his passion and enthusiasm on the touchline and inspired Saints to victory in his first home match at the helm. Arsenal were 22 matches unbeaten and twice fought back after goals from Danny Ings, but Charlie Austin's header five minutes from time was the clincher.

SAINTS 2-1 TOTTENHAM

Hasenhüttl was less enthused by the first-half performance of his team against Spurs, who had just booked their place in the Champions League quarter-finals. A double substitution at the interval, by which time Saints were trailing, helped turn the tide, as Yan Valery and James Ward-Prowse struck in the final 15 minutes.

SAINTS 3-3 BOURNEMOUTH

One point was enough for Saints to celebrate survival, but both south coast neighbours tried everything to win this thriller in the sunshine. Shane Long continued his fine form with the opener, but the hosts trailed 2-1 before James Ward-Prowse's daisy-cutter, while Matt Targett's header briefly had Saints on course for 40 points.

LEICESTER 1-2 SAINTS

A result that propelled Saints out of the relegation zone after a superhuman effort with ten men. James Ward-Prowse fired the visitors in front from the penalty spot, but things looked bleak when Yan Valery was sent off before half time. Shane Long instantly doubled the lead, before Saints survived a second-half onslaught.

MAN UTD 3-2 SAINTS

Not the desired outcome, but proof Saints now had a team capable of competing with the best. United were the Premier League's form team, and recovered from Yan Valery's wonder goal to lead. Another special strike – this time a James Ward-Prowse free-kick – looked to have earned a point before Romelu Lukaku's late winner.

SAINT LONG: RECORD BREAKER!

On Tuesday 23rd April 2019 at Vicarage Road, Watford, Saints striker Shane Long wrote his name into the Premier League history books by scoring the competition's fastest-ever goal. Clocking in at 7.69 seconds, the Irishman shattered the previous record, which had stood for 19 years...

7 STEPS TO 7TH HEAVEN IN 7 SECONDS!

0:12 With other players flat-footed, Long is ready and waiting to burst forward as Watford's Roberto Pereyra takes the kick-off.

3:26 As defender Craig Cathcart receives the ball and prepares to play forward, Long makes himself as big as he can to make a block.

4:23 When Cathcart's clearance strikes him on the back, Long is quickest to react and sprints towards the loose ball.

5:63 Just getting there first, Long crucially takes his first touch across the defender, who cannot risk a foul that could lead to a red card.

6:61 Breaking into the penalty area, Long assesses the position of goalkeeper Ben Foster and decides how he will finish the chance.

6:90 With Foster going to ground, Long opts to lift the ball over his former West Brom teammate. Will it find its target?

7:69 You bet! The ball drops just inside the near post and Long wheels away in celebration, unaware of the record he's just broken.

How YOU reacted...

Edward Marsh @edwardmarshCT — Follow
Replying to @SouthamptonFC
SHUTTTT UPPPP 😀😀😀 ● ●
7:47 PM - 23 Apr 2019

Tanmay @foreversaint_ — Follow
Replying to @SouthamptonFC
Wow can you just not wait for me.
7:46 PM - 23 Apr 2019

Kev @footy_mad — Follow
Replying to @SouthamptonFC
I think Shane is making a late run for the Golden boot......... if he keeps scoring every 8 seconds until the end of the season he may get it !!!!!!!!
8:07 PM - 23 Apr 2019
10 Likes

VixyLoveRocket @BustySantaClara — Follow
Replying to @SouthamptonFC
Got to be a record surely! #saintsfc
7:47 PM - 23 Apr 2019
2 Likes

Matt @Matty_Minnis — Follow
Replying to @SouthamptonFC
We now have fastest goal and fastest hat trick!
8:37 PM - 23 Apr 2019

Tony Wilde @TonyWilde99 — Follow
Replying to @SouthamptonFC
That didn't take Long
7:49 PM - 23 Apr 2019
45 Likes

Adam @LonerAnthem — Follow
Replying to @SouthamptonFC
What is life right now
7:48 PM - 23 Apr 2019

JBsRednWhiteSFC @SailorGirl30 — Follow
Replying to @SouthamptonFC
What a beauty of a goal, thank you Shane!!
9:55 PM - 23 Apr 2019
2 Likes

thisisalloneword @thisisall1word — Follow
Replying to @SouthamptonFC
That's about the long and short of it. COYR
8:30 PM - 23 Apr 2019
1 Like

How WE reacted...

LONG SCORES AFTER 7 SECONDS
ME: "DON'T SAY IT, DON'T SAY IT, DON'T SAY IT, DON'T SAY IT, DON'T SAY IT..."

View Insights — Promote
Liked by yan.valery and 16,331 others
southamptonfc ALSO ME: WELL THAT DIDN'T TAKE SHANE LONG. #saintsfc #premierleague

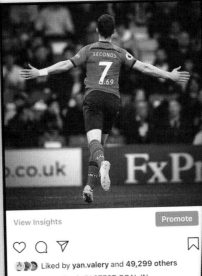

View Insights — Promote
Liked by yan.valery and 49,299 others
southamptonfc ⚡ FASTEST GOAL IN @premierleague HISTORY FROM SHANE LONG ⚡ #saintsfc

View Insights — Promote
6,437 likes
southamptonfc I C O N I C: Where were you when Shane Long made @premierleague history on Tuesday night? #saintsfc

5 fastest Prem goals EVER...

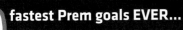

1 — 07.69 **SHANE LONG**
Watford vs SAINTS, 2019

2 — 09.82 **LEDLEY KING**
Bradford vs SPURS, 2000

3 — 10.52 **ALAN SHEARER**
NEWCASTLE vs Man City, 2003

4 — 10.54 **CHRISTIAN ERIKSEN**
SPURS vs Man Utd, 2018

5 — 11.90 **MARK VIDUKA**
Charlton vs LEEDS, 2001

DID YOU KNOW...

It's not the first time Saints have scored in record time... Sadio Mané's hat-trick against Aston Villa at St Mary's in May 2015 is still the fastest EVER in the Premier League at a staggering **2 MINUTES 56 SECONDS!** Which record will stand for the longest?

THE SEASON

9
GOALS SCORED BY NATHAN REDMOND, SAINTS' TOP SCORER IN ALL COMPETITIONS

6
ASSISTS FROM NATHAN REDMOND, SAINTS' MOST PROLIFIC PROVIDER IN 2018/19

2
PREMIER LEAGUE PLAYER OF THE MONTH NOMINATIONS FOR JAMES WARD-PROWSE

4
GOALS SCORED IN APRIL BY SHANE LONG, WHO PREVIOUSLY HAD ONE GOAL ALL SEASON

43
NATHAN REDMOND WAS THE ONLY SAINT TO PLAY ALL 43 GAMES IN ALL COMPETITIONS

18 YEARS 169 DAYS
MICHAEL OBAFEMI'S AGE WHEN HE BECAME SAINTS' YOUNGEST EVER PL GOALSCORER

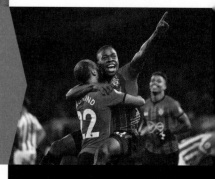

238
AVERAGE TIME IN MINUTES BETWEEN DANNY INGS'S PL GOALS – SAINTS' BEST RATIO

1.30
SAINTS' POINTS PER GAME UNDER RALPH HASENHÜTTL, WHICH WAS PREVIOUSLY 0.53

2
PIERRE-EMILE HØJBJERG WAS ONE OF ONLY TWO PL PLAYERS TO BE SENT OFF TWICE

11
ORIOL ROMEU WAS THE ONLY SAINT IN DOUBLE FIGURES FOR YELLOW CARDS RECEIVED

1,793
PASSES COMPLETED BY PIERRE-EMILE HØJBJERG, FAR BEYOND ANY OF HIS TEAMMATES

9
CLEAN SHEETS KEPT BY SAINTS IN ALL COMPETITIONS (MCCARTHY FOUR, GUNN FIVE)

IN NUMBERS

70
AVERAGE NUMBER OF SECONDS BETWEEN EACH TIME PIERRE-EMILE HØJBJERG HAD POSSESSION

74
SHOTS ATTEMPTED BY NATHAN REDMOND IN THE PL – JUST UNDER TWO PER GAME

3,278
PL MINUTES PLAYED BY NATHAN REDMOND – SAINTS' SECOND HIGHEST WAS 2,764

81
TACKLES WON BY ORIOL ROMEU – 10 MORE THAN PIERRE-EMILE HØJBJERG IN SECOND PLACE

171
CLEARANCES BY SAINTS' JANNIK VESTERGAARD – JUST AHEAD OF JAN BEDNAREK (168)

78
SAVES MADE BY ALEX MCCARTHY IN 25 APPEARANCES – MORE THAN THREE PER GAME

71
INTERCEPTIONS BY JAN BEDNAREK, WHO ALSO REGISTERED A SAINTS HIGH OF 27 BLOCKS

145
CROSSES ATTEMPTED BY JAMES WARD-PROWSE – THE ONLY SAINT IN THREE FIGURES

14,297
PASSES COMPLETED BY SAINTS ACROSS THE PL SEASON, AVERAGING 376 PER GAME

61%
AERIAL DUELS WON BY JANNIK VESTERGAARD, WHO USED HIS HEIGHT TO GOOD EFFECT

5
SAINTS ACADEMY GRADUATES WHO MADE THEIR FIRST-TEAM DEBUTS IN 2018/19

13
UNLUCKY FOR SOME – THE NUMBER OF TIMES SAINTS HIT THE WOODWORK

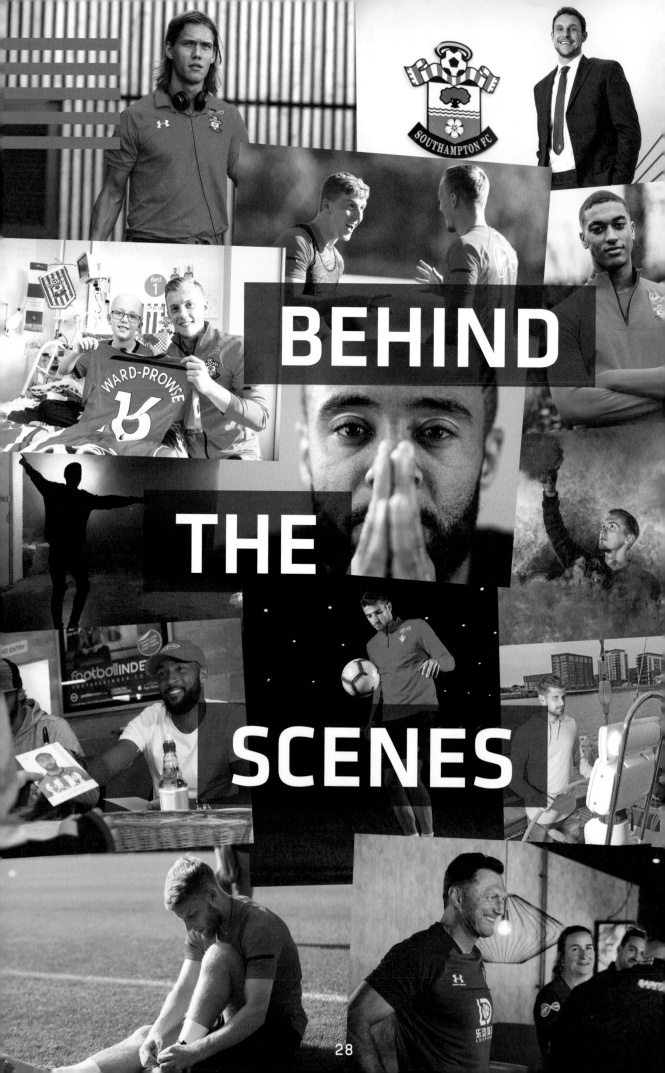

BEHIND THE SCENES

WITH THE SAINTS!

ANGUS GUNN'S 5 TIPS TO PENALTY-SAVING GLORY

England Under-21 keeper Angus Gunn has already established a reputation for saving penalties. First, he thwarted former Saint Theo Walcott in the Carabao Cup shoot-out win over Everton, before adding global superstar Paul Pogba to his list of victims at Old Trafford. Here, we ask him for some handy pointers to help out any aspiring shot-stoppers...

1▶ Know your opponent

I'm lucky to have video analysis on my side, but you can also pick up clues from the way they strike the ball – what's their technique like? Do they have a favourite corner when they shoot?

2▶ Disrupt their routine

Get your hands on the ball, move on your line, make yourself big, touch the crossbar... if you know they prefer one corner, leave a bigger gap on that side and get into their head a bit.

3▶ Make eye contact

Are they nervous or confident? If they look confident, they might look at the opposite corner to fool you. If they look nervous, they're more likely to focus on the corner they're aiming for.

4▶ Assess the run-up

If it's a straighter run-up, they're probably going to open their foot out, but if it's more of an angled run-up, they're more likely to cut it across their body.

5▶ Time it right – or left?

Diving too early makes it too easy for the taker, but too late and you'll struggle to reach the corner. Wait until their last step and dive as far as you can – even if it's not right in the corner, you should still save it with your body or your legs.

GK Q&A

Goalkeeping hero?

Petr Čech. When he first came to the Premier League he was unbelievable, and the way he came back from serious injury was inspiring.

Best in the world?

Buffon has been at the top for ages, but the likes of Courtois and Oblak are coming through now. When they win more trophies, they'll get more accolades.

Shoot-out specialist?

I think I prefer the taller goalkeepers in a penalty shoot-out. If it was Real Madrid against Barcelona, I'd probably back Courtois just because of the size of him!

Keepers love penalties... true or false?

True! The pressure is on the taker and even if you only save one, you can be the hero. It's the biggest chance for keepers to be in the spotlight.

Favourite penalty save?

The one from Walcott in the Carabao Cup, and also against Dortmund in pre-season when I was at Man City. It was Guardiola's first game in charge.

Always played in goal?

I started outfield, but I went in goal when I was about eight. You never know until you try it, and I've been there ever since!

MEET THE DEBUTANTS

TYREKE JOHNSON

Nationality:
English
Position:
Left winger
PL Debut:
vs Arsenal (H), 16/12/2018
Age on Debut:
20 years, 1 month, 13 days

Who do you look up to most in the squad?

TJ: Nathan Redmond. I like the way he plays – he's direct, he creates chances for the team and works hard off the ball.

CS: Nathan Redmond gives me a lot of advice every day, so I take that on board and use it to my advantage. He's spoken to me about moving the ball quickly, and how to grow into a game.

YV: Mario Lemina is like a big brother to me – not only because he speaks French, but because he takes care of me when I've got problems. As a footballer, he's a really good player – he played in the Champions League final with Juventus.

KR: There's a few, so I couldn't really pick one. The most helpful players to me have been James Ward-Prowse, Jack Stephens, Pierre-Emile Højbjerg and Ryan Bertrand.

What is the best advice you have been given?

TJ: Be patient, because you never know when your chance is going to come. When it does, you need to be ready to take that opportunity.

CS: Believe in your own ability. If you believe in your own ability, you can always achieve what you're capable of.

YV: You will always make mistakes in your life, but when you do make a mistake you have to keep going and stay confident.

KR: No matter what's going on around you, always give 100 per cent because you never know who's watching.

CALLUM SLATTERY

Nationality:
English
Position:
Central midfielder
PL Debut:
vs Leicester (A), 12/01/2019
Age on Debut:
19 years, 11 months, 4 days

YAN VALERY

Nationality:
French

Position:
Right-back

PL Debut:
vs Man United (H), 01/12/2018

Age on Debut:
19 years, 9 months, 9 days

What area of your game needs the most improvement?

TJ: I think I need to work on my weaker foot. I'm a bit too left-footed at the moment!

CS: Physically, I would say my speed. With the ball, I still need a bit more cutting edge to my game in the final third so I can score more goals.

YV: I would say the two main things would be my heading technique, and seeing what's in front of me before I receive the ball.

KR: I would definitely say staying switched on for the full 90 minutes. As a defender, it's so important to stay focused and sense danger.

KAYNE RAMSAY

Nationality:
English

Position:
Right-back

PL Debut:
vs Man City (H), 30/12/2018

Age on Debut:
18 years, 2 months, 20 days

What is your best footballing attribute?

TJ: Probably my crossing. I think I've got a good delivery that can help create chances for other players. It's something that comes quite naturally to me, but I still practise it to keep improving.

CS: Seeing a pass – I think that's what I'm best at. I don't know if you can really work on it, but it's just something I've always done. I try to see a pass out of the corner of my eye and execute it.

YV: I'm powerful and quick. I've always had that since I was young, but it's also something I keep working hard to improve in the gym and on the training pitch.

KR: My athleticism. I've always been a good one-on-one defender, but since I've come to Southampton I've become more attacking, so I'm using that athleticism to get up and down the pitch.

SOUTHAMPTON UNDER-23S:

Success at Academy level can be difficult to quantify; is it results on the pitch, or players progressing to the first team? In 2018/19, Saints achieved both, with five graduates making their senior debuts alongside success for the Under-18s, who finished fourth in the Premier League, and the Under-23s, who secured promotion back to the top flight...

PREMIER LEAGUE 2 DIVISION 2 FINAL TABLE

		Pld	W	D	L	GD	Pts
1	Wolves	22	13	4	5	23	43
2	**SAINTS**	22	13	4	5	16	43
3	Reading	22	12	4	6	12	40
4	Newcastle United	22	13	1	8	9	40
5	Aston Villa	22	11	4	7	5	37
6	Manchester United	22	8	6	8	2	30
7	Stoke City	22	7	7	8	5	28
8	Middlesbrough	22	6	8	8	-4	26
9	West Bromwich Albion	22	5	9	8	-5	24
10	Fulham	22	5	7	10	-8	22
11	Norwich City	22	5	4	13	-22	19
12	Sunderland	22	2	6	14	-33	12

WOLVES WON THE LEAGUE ON GOAL DIFFERENCE, MEANING SAINTS ENTERED THE END OF SEASON PLAY-OFFS...

> **SEMI-FINAL 1** Reading 2-2 Newcastle United AET (Newcastle win 3-2 on penalties)
>
> **SEMI-FINAL 2** Saints 2-0 Aston Villa (Smallbone pen, O'Connor)
>
> **FINAL** Saints 2-1 Newcastle United (N'Lundulu, Johnson)

WE SAID...

"I'm really, really pleased with the boys' performance throughout the season – the way they've matured and improved in many aspects – but I said to them, we need to finish it off and win something. That will stay in our memories and make a legacy for them before they either go into the first team here, or somewhere else." *Radhi Jaïdi, Southampton Under-23s Coach*

PLAY-OFF WINNERS!

UNDER-18 PREMIER LEAGUE SOUTH FINAL TABLE

		Pld	W	D	L	GD	Pts
1	Arsenal	22	20	0	2	63	60
2	Tottenham Hotspur	22	18	2	2	55	56
3	Chelsea	22	13	5	4	18	44
4	**SAINTS**	**22**	**11**	**2**	**9**	**7**	**35**
5	Brighton and Hove Albion	22	11	1	10	3	34
6	Aston Villa	22	9	2	11	-3	29
7	Leicester City	22	9	2	11	-9	29
8	West Ham United	22	9	2	11	-14	29
9	Fulham	22	6	6	10	-9	24
10	Reading	22	6	1	15	-31	19
11	Swansea City	22	3	3	16	-34	12
12	Norwich City	22	3	2	17	-46	11

WE SAID...

"We only had one point after five games played, so I'm very pleased with how the boys have responded. Radhi [Jaïdi] trusts the players we're passing on to him, and clearly the manager [Ralph Hasenhüttl] trusts the players moving up from the Under-23s. There's a great continuity going through the club." *Paul Hardyman, Southampton Under-18s Coach*

DID YOU KNOW?

Southampton Under-18s were the first visiting team to play at the new Tottenham Hotspur Stadium, as Saints faced their Spurs counterparts in a test event at the Londoners' new home in front of 28,987 spectators. Spurs ran out 3-1 winners, but Saints' Norwegian youngster Kornelius Hansen will forever be the first away player to score at the venue.

SOUTHAMPTON FC WOMEN

2018/19 was a season to cherish for Southampton FC Women, who completed a perfect league campaign with 18 wins out of 18 to be crowned Southern Region Women's Premier Division champions! As if that wasn't enough, the girls added the League Cup to their name to round off a memorable year!

DOUBLE WINNERS!

SOUTHERN REGION WOMEN'S FOOTBALL LEAGUE PREMIER DIVISION FINAL TABLE

		Pld	W	D	L	GD	Pts
1	**SOUTHAMPTON FC WOMEN**	18	18	0	0	86	54
2	AFC Bournemouth CST	18	16	0	2	77	48
3	Oxford City	18	13	0	5	25	39
4	Woodley United	18	8	3	7	-8	27
5	Warsash Wasps	18	7	1	10	-13	22
6	Ascot United	18	5	6	7	-15	21
7	Winchester City Flyers	18	5	1	12	-19	16
8	Newbury	18	4	1	13	-55	13
9	Barton Rovers	18	3	2	13	-37	11
10	New Milton Town	18	3	2	13	-41	10*

* Adjustment made to points

21 SCORED, 0 CONCEDED: SOUTHAMPTON FC WOMEN'S ROAD TO LEAGUE CUP GLORY...

FIRST ROUND Southampton FC Women 4-0 Moneyfields (Pusey 3, Freeland)

QUARTER-FINAL Wargrave 0-9 Southampton FC Women (Newton 5, Collighan 2, Woods, o.g.)

SEMI-FINAL Wycombe Wanderers 0-6 Southampton FC Women (Chaffe 3, Newton, Williams, Freeland)

FINAL Oxford City 0-2 Southampton FC Women (Williams, Pusey)

WE SAID... "We want the Southampton FC Women's team to be the groundbreaking team for the next group of girls to come in. The success is the people. The players are at university, they are at college, they are working and yet they come here week in, week out. The growth in them as individuals has been phenomenal." *Marieanne Spacey-Cale, Southampton FC Women Head Coach*

THE SAINTS STORE

From watches to dinosaurs and everything in between, check out our brilliant range of official Saints gear, available to buy online or at both the Stadium and Westquay stores now.

Sammy or Mary Plush Toy **£14**

Saints Lunch Bag **£12**

Saints T-Rex **£10**

Sammy Saint Notebook **£8**

Kit Stationery Set **£12**

Saints Pearl Football **£12**

Kids Saints Watch **£30**

Blaze Kids Backpack **£16**

 STADIUM & WESTQUAY STORES

 SOUTHAMPTONFC.COM

 OFFICIAL DISCOUNTS APPLY

BRXLZ St Mary's Stadium **£60**

Saints Colouring Book **£8**

SAINTS PUZZLES

CAN YOU ANSWER ALL 10 QUESTIONS CORRECTLY TO UNLOCK THE ANSWER?

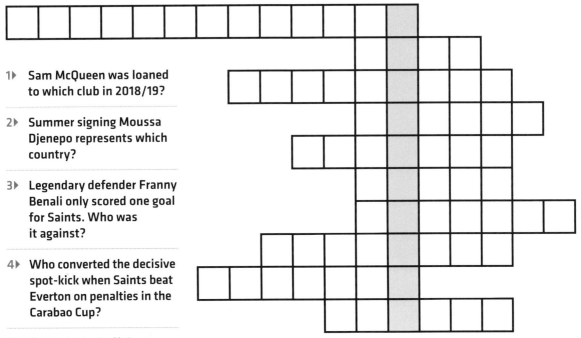

1▶ Sam McQueen was loaned to which club in 2018/19?

2▶ Summer signing Moussa Djenepo represents which country?

3▶ Legendary defender Franny Benali only scored one goal for Saints. Who was it against?

4▶ Who converted the decisive spot-kick when Saints beat Everton on penalties in the Carabao Cup?

5▶ Saints kicked off the 2018/19 and 2019/20 seasons against which club?

6▶ How many ex-Saints played in the 2019 Champions League final?

7▶ Saints manager Ralph Hasenhüttl hails from which country?

8▶ Which youngster made his first league start against Burnley in February 2019?

9▶ Which Saints legend scored on his England debut with his first touch in 2013?

10▶ Who made their Premier League bow in Mark Hughes's last game in charge?

NAME THAT SAINT!

These six Saints are all partially hidden... can you identify them?

Answers on page 60

MEET THE NEW BOYS

MOUSSA DJENEPO

MOUSSA SAID: "I analysed the situation a lot – I talked it over with my team and my family, and we decided Southampton was right for me. It's a place that can help me to progress."

RALPH SAID: "Moussa is an exciting player, with tremendous pace and good finishing abilities. We have been impressed with how he has adapted to football in Europe."

DID YOU KNOW?

Moussa is a client of '12Management' – a sports consultancy company founded by former Premier League striker Freddie Kanouté, who also hails from Mali.

FACTFILE

Date of Birth:	15/06/98
Position:	Winger
Height:	177cm
Weight:	65kg
Nationality:	Malian
Date Signed:	13/06/19
Contract:	2023
Signed From:	Standard Liège
2018/19 Stats:	37 apps, 11 goals
Career Stats:	54 apps, 12 goals
International:	13 caps, 1 goal

GETTING TO KNOW...
MOUSSA DJENEPO

Where did you grow up?
I had a nice childhood in Mali with my family.

What is your earliest football memory?
I used to watch football on TV and play a lot in the streets. I always enjoyed following the World Cup, AFCON and Champions League.

Who is your sporting hero?
I would have to say Ronaldinho. I loved his skills and tricks – he was an entertainer.

Can you play any other sports?
No, only football!

What music are you into?
I like Malian music – Malian rap is my favourite.

Who has been the biggest influence on your career?
My family help me a lot – all of them. They have always been very supportive.

Can you can cook?
Yes! I cook African food at home.

What is your favourite holiday destination?
I like to go back to Mali. My family are still there, so I get the chance to see them when I visit.

How would you describe your personality?
I'm simple – I'm not a complicated person. I smile all the time, I like to laugh and I am a happy guy.

MEET THE NEW BOYS

CHÉ ADAMS

CHÉ SAID: "With the amount of young players here, the gaffer's belief in the young players, and the squad itself, you can see where the club is going to be. I want to be part of that."

RALPH SAID: "Ché has shown a desire to join us above all other clubs, which shows the positive reputation Southampton has built for developing young players."

DID YOU KNOW?

Ché made his professional debut against Saints as a Sheffield United player, back in the 2014/15 League Cup quarter-finals.

FACTFILE

Date of Birth:	13/07/96
Position:	Forward
Height:	175cm
Weight:	70kg
Nationality:	English
Date Signed:	01/07/19
Contract:	2024
Signed From:	Birmingham
2018/19 Stats:	48 apps, 22 goals
Career Stats:	178 apps, 53 goals

GETTING TO KNOW...
CHÉ ADAMS

Where did you grow up?
Leicester.

What is your earliest football memory?
Playing against Tottenham for Sheffield United in the semi-finals of the League Cup and scoring two goals.

Who is your sporting hero?
Thierry Henry. I loved watching him when he was at Arsenal – he was a great player.

Can you play any other sports?
Does PlayStation count as a sport?! It's always been football for me – that's all I ever wanted to do.

What has been your career highlight so far?
Probably last season, ending on 22 goals in the Championship.

Who are the best players you have played with and against?
Against, I would say Mousa Dembélé for Tottenham in the cup. He was very good. And Harry Kane, too. With? It would have to be some of the lads here now, but I can't pick one yet!

Prior to signing for Saints, did you know any players already at the club?
I knew Sam Gallagher, who was on loan at Birmingham, but obviously he's now gone to Blackburn. Otherwise, just Nathan Redmond.

Who is the most famous person you've ever met?
Probably Drake, at one of his concerts last October.

How would you describe your personality?
Easy going, laid back, willing to work, humble and funny – hopefully!

MEET THE NEW BOYS

KEVIN DANSO

KEVIN SAID: "It's a boyhood dream of mine to play in the Premier League. I'm physically quite imposing, and I'm looking to bring that into the league against some of the top strikers."

RALPH SAID: "Kevin is in the early part of his career, but he has good experience already, with a lot of existing qualities and the potential to develop even further. He will improve our defensive options."

— DID YOU KNOW? —

One of the reasons Kevin chose to join Augsburg in Germany was because there was the option of an English-speaking school, where he could finish his A Levels.

FACTFILE

Date of Birth:	19/09/98
Position:	Defender
Height:	190cm
Weight:	87kg
Nationality:	Austrian
Date Signed:	09/08/19
Contract:	2020 (loan)
Signed From:	FC Augsburg
2018/19 Stats:	21 apps, 1 goal
Career Stats:	44 apps, 3 goals
International:	6 caps, 0 goals

GETTING TO KNOW...
KEVIN DANSO

Where did you grow up?
I was born in Austria and lived there until the age of six. Then I moved to Milton Keynes until I was 15, when I moved to Germany.

What is your earliest football memory?
Probably my brothers playing FIFA on the PS One, when you could foul the goalkeeper!

Who is your sporting hero?
I have quite a few, but Didier Drogba would be one. If not a footballer, Muhammad Ali. He changed sport as we know it, and he's definitely a role model for every sportsman.

Can you play any other sports?
I think I'm quite talented in other sports, if I may say so! I had the chance to play rugby on a scholarship at some private schools, but I chose football.

What has been your career highlight so far?
Probably my international debut for Austria or my Bundesliga debut for Augsburg. I will also add in the U21 Euros – the whole experience was something I'll never forget.

Who has been the biggest influence on your career?
My two brothers, who have been with me through everything.

Who are the best players you have played with and against?
If I had to say a few that were really surprising to me, I would say Marko Arnautović, Edinson Cavani, Robert Lewandowski and Thiago.

How would you describe your personality?
Very laid back, silly at times, but always focused when it comes down to it.

RALPH HASENHÜTTL

RALPH SAID: "I think no matter where I've worked, the stadiums have always been full as a result of how we played. It's successful, attractive and represents a particular way of life."

THEY SAID: "The football that he wants to play will be very much suited to the Premier League. It's all-action, high-pressing – almost anti-Pep Guardiola, is how I've described it." – *German football expert Archie Rhind-Tutt*

DID YOU KNOW?

Having been appointed in the summer after promotion, Ralph masterminded a runner-up finish for RB Leipzig in their first season in the Bundesliga, in 2016/17.

FACTFILE

Date of Birth:	09/08/67
Nationality:	Austrian
Date Appointed:	05/12/18
Contract:	2021
Previous Club:	RB Leipzig
Playing Position:	Forward
Playing Stats:	450 apps, 119 goals
International:	8 caps, 3 goals
Management Stats:	359 games, 152 wins (42%)

GETTING TO KNOW...
RALPH HASENHÜTTL

Ralph Hasenhüttl was appointed Southampton manager midway through the 2018/19 campaign with the club precariously positioned in the Premier League relegation zone, having won only one league game all season.

The league's first ever Austrian manager, Hasenhüttl watched from the stands at Wembley as Saints went down 3-1 to Tottenham, before overseeing a damaging 1-0 defeat to fellow strugglers Cardiff in his first game in charge.

But a first full week's training with his new players reaped instant rewards, as Saints stunned Arsenal at St Mary's, before tasting victory over Huddersfield, taking the team's tally to a previously unimaginable six goals in two games.

That was the turning point, as Saints embarked on a run of eight wins in 17 league outings, guaranteeing survival with two matches to spare.

Hasenhüttl's animated style on the touchline is reflected in his team's high-intensity approach on the pitch, both of which have made the new boss a big hit with the club's supporters.

Off the field, he has thrown himself into community events with Saints Foundation and organised open training sessions at St Mary's, helping to strengthen the bond between team and fans.

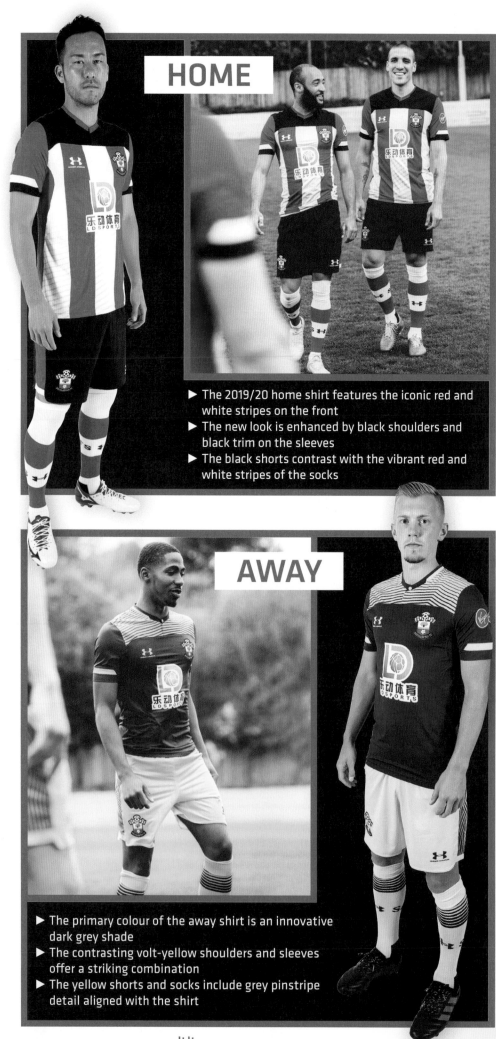

HOME

- The 2019/20 home shirt features the iconic red and white stripes on the front
- The new look is enhanced by black shoulders and black trim on the sleeves
- The black shorts contrast with the vibrant red and white stripes of the socks

AWAY

- The primary colour of the away shirt is an innovative dark grey shade
- The contrasting volt-yellow shoulders and sleeves offer a striking combination
- The yellow shorts and socks include grey pinstripe detail aligned with the shirt

GK HOME

► Saints' last line of defence wear sky blue from head to toe, with subtle black trim

GK AWAY

► The away version follows a similar theme, with the aprimary colour bright pink

THIRD

► The third kit is mainly white but replicates the pinstripe detail of the away shirt
► The colourful red and navy trim features on the shoulders, sleeves and shorts
► The secondary colour, navy, offers contrast as the primary colour of athe socks

THINK YOU COULD DO BETTER? DESIGN YOUR OWN!

19/20 MEMBERSHIP

BE AHEAD OF THE GAME

WITH PRIORITY TICKET ACCESS

PRICES FROM £25

OFFICIAL SAINT +	OFFICIAL SAINT	JUNIOR SAINT
£45	£35	£25

MEMBERSHIP INCLUDES

OFFICIAL SAINT +
- First priority access to all Premier League home games
- £5 off all category A-C fixtures - save up to £80
- First priority access to all away games (After Season Ticket Holders)

OFFICIAL SAINT
- Priority access to all Premier League home games (After Official Saint + Members)
- £5 off all category B&C fixtures - save up to £35
- Priority access to all away games (After Season Ticket Holders and Official Saint + Members)

JUNIOR SAINT
- First priority access to all Premier League home games
- 5% off retail both in store and online
- Official welcome pack and £1 tickets to our Junior matchday

 tickets.saintsfc.co.uk   02381 780 780

INTERNATIONAL SAINTS

Saints have a whole host of players who have played for their countries, but can you match the number of the correct statement with the player in question?

Alex McCarthy · Cédric · Danny Ings · Moussa Djenepo · James Ward-Prowse

Jan Bednarek · Jannik Vestergaard · Josh Sims · Maya Yoshida · Michael Obafemi

ohamed Elyounoussi · Nathan Redmond · Pierre-Emile Højbjerg · Shane Long · Stuart Armstrong

1. I scored a last-gasp equaliser for my country in a 2-2 draw against Kosovo in March 2019.
2. I represent the same country as the mystery goalscorer, but I went to the 2018 World Cup.
3. I made my England debut in November 2018, five and a half years after my first call-up.
4. My only England appearance to date was earned in my time as a Liverpool player.
5. I also have one Three Lions cap to my name, but was called up for a second time in 2019.
6. With 82 appearances for my country, I am the most-capped player at Southampton.
7. At the other end of the spectrum, I made my debut for the same country in November 2018.
8. I joined up late with Saints' pre-season plans because I was playing in the Africa Cup of Nations.
9. I was born in Africa, but chose to play my international football for a European country.
10. I took time out of the 2018/19 Premier League season to lead my country to the Asian Cup final.
11. I am a champion of my own continent from 2016 – the highlight of my professional career.
12. Signing for Saints in 2017 gave me the perfect platform to earn international recognition.
13. I was given my international debut by the manager who led Saints to the 2003 FA Cup final.
14. I won the U17 Euros with England, but missed the U20 World Cup triumph in 2017 with injury.
15. I won my second England cap in March 2019, virtually two years to the day after my first.

Answers on page 60

1
ALEX MCCARTHY

Date of Birth: **03/12/89**
Position: **Goalkeeper**
Height: **193cm**
Weight: **79kg**
Nationality: **English**
2018/19: **25 apps,**
4 clean sheets

Did You Know?
Made his long-awaited England debut five and a half years after his first call-up.

2
CÉDRIC

Date of Birth: **31/08/91**
Position: **Defender**
Height: **172cm**
Weight: **67kg**
Nationality: **Portuguese**
2018/19: **22 apps,**
1 goal

Did You Know?
Scored his first PL goal on his 100th appearance in the competition.

3
MAYA YOSHIDA

Date of Birth: **24/08/88**
Position: **Defender**
Height: **189cm**
Weight: **78kg**
Nationality: **Japanese**
2018/19: **20 apps,**
0 goals

Did You Know?
Donates one per cent of his salary to Saints Foundation's work in the community.

4
JANNIK VESTERGAARD

Date of Birth: **03/08/92**
Position: **Defender**
Height: **199cm**
Weight: **96kg**
Nationality: **Danish**
2018/19: **26 apps,**
0 goals

Did You Know?
His pet dog, Brady, is named after the legendary NFL quarterback Tom Brady.

5
JACK STEPHENS

Date of Birth: **27/01/94**
Position: **Defender**
Height: **185cm**
Weight: **75kg**
Nationality: **English**
2018/19: **29 apps,**
1 goal

Did You Know?
As a youngster in Plymouth's Academy, he would commute to training by ferry.

6
WESLEY HOEDT

Date of Birth: **06/03/94**
Position: **Defender**
Height: **188cm**
Weight: **77kg**
Nationality: **Dutch**
2018/19: **13 apps,**
0 goals

Did You Know?
Made his Netherlands debut in 2017, coming on as sub for Matthijs de Ligt.

7
SHANE
LONG

Date of Birth: **22/01/87**
Position: **Forward**
Height: **178cm**
Weight: **70kg**
Nationality: **Irish**
2018/19: **28 apps,**
5 goals

Did You Know?
Became only the fourth Irishman to score 50 goals in the Premier League.

9
DANNY
INGS

Date of Birth: **23/07/92**
Position: **Forward**
Height: **178cm**
Weight: **73kg**
Nationality: **English**
2018/19: **25 apps,**
8 goals

Did You Know?
Scored Saints' first goal under Ralph Hasenhüttl en route to a brace against Arsenal.

11
MOHAMED
ELYOUNOUSSI

Date of Birth: **04/08/94**
Position: **Winger**
Height: **178cm**
Weight: **70kg**
Nationality: **Norwegian**
2018/19: **19 apps,**
0 goals

Did You Know?
Played under Manchester United manager Ole Gunnar Solskjaer at Molde.

14
ORIOL
ROMEU

Date of Birth: **24/09/91**
Position: **Midfielder**
Height: **183cm**
Weight: **83kg**
Nationality: **Spanish**
2018/19: **33 apps,**
1 goal

Did You Know?
Made his international debut for Catalonia against Venezuela in March 2019.

16
JAMES
WARD-PROWSE

Date of Birth: **01/11/94**
Position: **Midfielder**
Height: **173cm**
Weight: **66kg**
Nationality: **English**
2018/19: **29 apps,**
7 goals

Did You Know?
Scored in three successive PL games on two separate occasions in 2018/19.

17
STUART
ARMSTRONG

Date of Birth: **30/03/92**
Position: **Midfielder**
Height: **183cm**
Weight: **75kg**
Nationality: **Scottish**
2018/19: **32 apps,**
4 goals

Did You Know?
Spent five years studying a law degree alongside his professional football career.

18
MARIO
LEMINA

Date of Birth: **01/09/93**
Position: **Midfielder**
Height: **184cm**
Weight: **85kg**
Nationality: **Gabonese**
2018/19: **23 apps,**
1 goals

Did You Know?
Plays international football as a teammate of Pierre-Emerick Aubameyang.

19
SOFIANE
BOUFAL

Date of Birth: **17/09/93**
Position: **Midfielder**
Height: **175cm**
Weight: **70kg**
Nationality: **Moroccan**
2018/19: **0 apps,**
0 goals

Did You Know?
Played alongside Wesley Hoedt on loan at Spanish club Celta Vigo in 2018/19.

20
MICHAEL OBAFEMI

Date of Birth: **06/07/00**
Position: **Forward**
Height: **169cm**
Weight: **71kg**
Nationality: **Irish**
2018/19: **7 apps, 1 goal**

Did You Know?
Saints' youngest-ever Premier League goalscorer at 18 years and 169 days old.

21
RYAN BERTRAND

Date of Birth: **05/08/89**
Position: **Defender**
Height: **179cm**
Weight: **85kg**
Nationality: **English**
2018/19: **24 apps, 1 goal**

Did You Know?
His goal against Leicester was his first at St Mary's since the 2015/16 season.

22
NATHAN REDMOND

Date of Birth: **06/03/94**
Position: **Winger**
Height: **173cm**
Weight: **69kg**
Nationality: **English**
2018/19: **43 apps, 9 goals**

Did You Know?
All nine of his goals – a career best for one season – were scored in the final 23 games.

23
PIERRE-EMILE HØJBJERG

Date of Birth: **05/08/95**
Position: **Midfielder**
Height: **185cm**
Weight: **84kg**
Nationality: **Danish**
2018/19: **33 apps, 4 goals**

Did You Know?
Once the youngest player ever to represent Bayern Munich in the Bundesliga.

25
GUIDO CARRILLO

Date of Birth: **25/05/91**
Position: **Forward**
Height: **188cm**
Weight: **87kg**
Nationality: **Argentinian**
2018/19: **0 apps, 0 goals**

Did You Know?
Was reunited with former Saints boss Mauricio Pellegrino on loan at Leganés.

28
ANGUS GUNN

Date of Birth: **22/01/96**
Position: **Goalkeeper**
Height: **196cm**
Weight: **77kg**
Nationality: **English**
2018/19: **17 apps, 5 clean sheets**

Did You Know?
Father Bryan was a Scottish international goalkeeper in the 1990s.

30
CALLUM SLATTERY

Date of Birth: **08/02/99**
Position: **Midfielder**
Height: **175cm**
Weight: **70kg**
Nationality: **English**
2018/19: **5 apps,**
0 goals

Did You Know?
Saints were undefeated in the five first-team games in which he featured.

31
KAYNE RAMSAY

Date of Birth: **10/10/00**
Position: **Defender**
Height: **179cm**
Weight: **66kg**
Nationality: **English**
2018/19: **2 apps,**
0 goals

Did You Know?
Became the youngest Premier League starter in 2018/19 at the time of his debut.

35
JAN BEDNAREK

Date of Birth: **12/04/96**
Position: **Defender**
Height: **189cm**
Weight: **77kg**
Nationality: **Polish**
2018/19: **27 apps,**
0 goals

Did You Know?
Older brother Filip is a goalkeeper for Dutch top-flight side SC Heerenveen.

41
HARRY LEWIS

Date of Birth: **20/12/97**
Position: **Goalkeeper**
Height: **191cm**
Weight: **77kg**
Nationality: **English**
2018/19: **0 apps,**
0 clean sheets

Did You Know?
Signed from Shrewsbury, where grandfather Ken Mulhearn starred in the 70s.

42
JAKE HESKETH

Date of Birth: **27/03/96**
Position: **Midfielder**
Height: **168cm**
Weight: **63kg**
Nationality: **English**
2018/19: **0 apps,**
0 goals

Did You Know?
Scored the winner for Burton against Middlesbrough in the EFL Cup quarter-finals.

43
YAN VALERY

Date of Birth: **22/02/99**
Position: **Defender**
Height: **183cm**
Weight: **79kg**
Nationality: **French**
2018/19: **24 apps,**
2 goals

Did You Know?
Scored his first two senior goals in successive games, against Man Utd and Spurs.

44
FRASER FORSTER

Date of Birth: **17/03/88**
Position: **Goalkeeper**
Height: **201cm**
Weight: **93kg**
Nationality: **English**
2018/19: **1 app,**
0 clean sheets

Did You Know?
Broke a Scottish league record at Celtic by going 1,256 minutes without conceding.

45
SAM MCQUEEN

Date of Birth: **06/02/95**
Position: **Defender**
Height: **181cm**
Weight: **70kg**
Nationality: **English**
2018/19: **0 apps,**
0 goals

Did You Know?
Helped Middlesbrough keep five clean sheets in seven games before injury.

TALE OF THE TENS

It's been quite a decade for Saints, from League One to the Europa League and everything in between...

Having started the season with a ten-point deduction, Saints kicked off 2010 in the bottom half of League One. On January 2nd, the team played their first match of the decade against Luton Town in the FA Cup third round. Fittingly, Rickie Lambert scored the only goal to send Saints through.

The first major high of the decade arrived on March 28th 2010, when more than 40,000 Saints fans witnessed the club secure its first piece of silverware in 34 years. Goals from Lambert, Adam Lallana, Papa Waigo and Michail Antonio secured a 4-1 victory over Carlisle United in the Football League Trophy final.

At the start of the 2010/11 campaign, the club was rocked by the shocking passing of owner Markus Liebherr at the age 62. On the field, manager Alan Pardew was sacked before the end of August, paving the way for Nigel Adkins to lay the foundations for Saints' return to the top tier.

A stunning late run of 13 wins from the last 15 games of the season saw Saints secure their return to the Championship. With names like Kelvin Davis, José Fonte, Morgan Schneiderlin, Lallana and Lambert in their ranks, Saints had formed the basis of a formidable spine.

Saints had built a talented squad led by an inspirational manager, and the positive momentum of promotion continued into the new campaign. Saints were riding the crest of a wave, as Lambert's 31 goals in 2011/12 helped the team sail straight through the Championship at the first attempt.

Back in the Premier League, Adkins was replaced by up and coming Argentinian manager Mauricio Pochettino midway through a first season in which Saints consolidated their place among English football's elite.

Pochettino's only full season at the helm proved a major success. Saints combined some slick attacking play with a rock-solid defence, going toe to toe with some of the best teams in the top flight, losing only one of their first 11 league games, including a 1-0 victory over Liverpool at Anfield.

After Pochettino departed for Tottenham, Ronald Koeman was appointed in summer 2014. Sunderland were thrashed 8-0, Manchester United beaten at Old Trafford and Sadio Mané scored the fastest-ever Premier League hat-trick in a season in which Saints occupied a Champions League place as late as February.

Koeman's team, which had seen the likes of Lambert and Lallana replaced by overseas stars Graziano Pellè, Dušan Tadić and Mané, finished sixth in 2015/16, Saints' highest top-flight finish in more than 30 years, overcoming the disappointment of losing out in Europa League qualifying, as the club ended a 12-year exile from European competition.

When Koeman left to manage Everton, Claude Puel would be his successor. The Frenchman oversaw a gruelling 53-game campaign in which Saints registered an historic win over Inter Milan and reached the League Cup final, where a gallant performance went unrewarded in a heartbreaking 3-2 defeat to Manchester United.

Saints opted to replace Puel after a poor end to the season, but replacement Mauricio Pellegrino was unable to halt the slide, leaving Mark Hughes to step in and help preserve the club's Premier League status with a nerve-shredding 1-0 win at Swansea. Virgil van Dijk became the world's most expensive defender in leaving for Liverpool in January 2018.

When Hughes struggled to build on survival, Ralph Hasenhüttl was appointed in December 2018 and soon made his presence felt, bringing life to St Mary's with dramatic home wins over Arsenal and Tottenham. Hasenhüttl's high tempo, pressing style was characterised by Shane Long scoring in just 7.69 seconds at Watford.

MEET THE OPPOSITION

AFC BOURNEMOUTH ....

Nickname: The Cherries
Ground: Vitality Stadium
Capacity: 11,364
Manager: Eddie Howe
Last Season: 14th
Star Player: Callum Wilson
Key Signing: Harry Wilson (Liverpool, loan)

VERDICT:
Bournemouth tend to start well and fade. Sustain their usual early season form and they can challenge for a top-half finish.

ARSENAL...

Nickname: The Gunners
Ground: Emirates Stadium
Capacity: 60,704
Manager: Unai Emery
Last Season: 5th
Star Player: Pierre-Emerick Aubameyang
Key Signing: Nicolas Pépé (Lille)

VERDICT:
After an unusually big-spending summer, Arsenal must target the top four and a return to the Champions League.

ASTON VILLA ....

Nickname: The Villans
Ground: Villa Park
Capacity: 42,095
Manager: Dean Smith
Last Season: 5th in Championship (play-off winners)
Star Player: Jack Grealish
Key Signing: Tom Heaton (Burnley)

VERDICT:
Some have accused Villa of 'doing a Fulham' and signing too many players, but they should stay up relatively comfortably.

BRIGHTON & HOVE ALBION...............

Nickname: The Seagulls
Ground: Amex Stadium
Capacity: 30,750
Manager: Graham Potter
Last Season: 17th
Star Player: Lewis Dunk
Key Signing: Leandro Trossard (Genk)

VERDICT:
Tough to expect much more than survival, but doing so by playing more attractive football is the task of new boss Potter.

BURNLEY.............................

Nickname:	The Clarets
Ground:	Turf Moor
Capacity:	21,944
Manager:	Sean Dyche
Last Season:	15th
Star Player:	Dwight McNeil
Key Signing:	Jay Rodriguez (West Brom)

VERDICT:
Last season's Europa League hangover affected their early results, but Burnley should stay clear of danger this time around.

CHELSEA ....

Nickname:	The Blues
Ground:	Stamford Bridge
Capacity:	40,834
Manager:	Frank Lampard
Last Season:	3rd
Star Player:	N'Golo Kanté
Key Signing:	Christian Pulisic (Dortmund)

VERDICT:
This is a really tough job for Lampard, who will hope to challenge for the top four but is likely to fall short without Eden Hazard.

CRYSTAL PALACE ....

Nickname:	The Eagles
Ground:	Selhurst Park
Capacity:	25,486
Manager:	Roy Hodgson
Last Season:	12th
Star Player:	Wilfried Zaha
Key Signing:	Gary Cahill (Chelsea)

VERDICT:
This could be a difficult season for Palace, but keeping hold of Zaha should be enough to guarantee survival at least.

EVERTON.............................

Nickname:	The Toffees
Ground:	Goodison Park
Capacity:	39,414
Manager:	Marco Silva
Last Season:	8th
Star Player:	Gylfi Sigurdsson
Key Signing:	Moise Kean (Juventus)

VERDICT:
It's time for Everton to seriously challenge for a place in the top six – if not, Silva could come under some serious pressure.

LEICESTER CITY ....

Nickname:	The Foxes
Ground:	King Power Stadium
Capacity:	32,261
Manager:	Brendan Rodgers
Last Season:	9th
Star Player:	James Maddison
Key Signing:	Youri Tielemans (Monaco)

VERDICT:
Another club with designs on gatecrashing the top six after Rodgers's impressive start, but Harry Maguire is a big loss.

LIVERPOOL ....

Nickname:	The Reds
Ground:	Anfield
Capacity:	53,394
Manager:	Jürgen Klopp
Last Season:	Runners-up
Star Player:	Mohamed Salah
Key Signing:	Harvey Elliott (Fulham)

VERDICT:
Can they go one better? When 97 points isn't enough, it's tough to see how Liverpool can leapfrog Manchester City.

MANCHESTER CITY ....

Nickname:	The Citizens
Ground:	Etihad Stadium
Capacity:	55,017
Manager:	Pep Guardiola
Last Season:	Champions
Star Player:	Kevin De Bruyne
Key Signing:	Rodri (Atlético Madrid)

VERDICT:
Rightly odds-on to secure a third successive Premier League title, but can City finally conquer the Champions League?

MANCHESTER UNITED.......................

Nickname:	The Red Devils
Ground:	Old Trafford
Capacity:	74,879
Manager:	Ole Gunnar Solskjaer
Last Season:	6th
Star Player:	Marcus Rashford
Key Signing:	Harry Maguire (Leicester)

VERDICT:
Depends if Solskjaer can rekindle the form of his first three months in charge – if so, a top-four finish should be theirs.

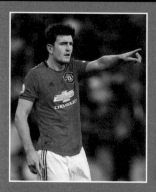

NEWCASTLE UNITED.........................

Nickname:	The Magpies
Ground:	St James' Park
Capacity:	52,305
Manager:	Steve Bruce
Last Season:	13th
Star Player:	Sean Longstaff
Key Signing:	Joelinton (Hoffenheim)

VERDICT:
Rafael Benítez did wonders with a limited squad, so if Bruce can keep Newcastle in the top flight, he's done well.

NORWICH CITY...............................

Nickname:	The Canaries
Ground:	Carrow Road
Capacity:	27,359
Manager:	Daniel Farke
Last Season:	Championship champions
Star Player:	Teemu Pukki
Key Signing:	Josip Drmić (Mönchengladbach)

VERDICT:
Rank outsiders along with Sheffield United, but should create chances and can stay up with strong enough home form.

SHEFFIELD UNITED ....

Nickname:	The Blades
Ground:	Bramall Lane
Capacity:	32,125
Manager:	Chris Wilder
Last Season:	Championship runners-up
Star Player:	Oliver Norwood
Key Signing:	Dean Henderson (Man Utd, loan)

VERDICT:
Even 17th would be a remarkable achievement, but the Blades will cause problems with their inventive style of play.

TOTTENHAM HOTSPUR.......................

Nickname:	Spurs
Ground:	Tottenham Hotspur Stadium
Capacity:	62,062
Manager:	Mauricio Pochettino
Last Season:	4th
Star Player:	Harry Kane
Key Signing:	Tanguy Ndombele (Lyon)

VERDICT:
Man City and Liverpool were so dominant last season, but Spurs are good enough to make it a three-horse race this time around.

WATFORD ....

Nickname:	The Hornets
Ground:	Vicarage Road
Capacity:	22,200
Manager:	Javi Gracia
Last Season:	11th
Star Player:	Gerard Deulofeu
Key Signing:	Ismaïla Sarr (Rennes)

VERDICT:
Watford were seventh with three games to go last season, but it's tough to see them challenging for Europe again.

WEST HAM UNITED.........................

Nickname:	The Hammers
Ground:	London Stadium
Capacity:	60,000
Manager:	Manuel Pellegrini
Last Season:	10th
Star Player:	Felipe Anderson
Key Signing:	Sébastien Haller (Frankfurt)

VERDICT:
After a succession of mid-table finishes, it's imperative Pellegrini takes West Ham to the next level after some big spending.

WOLVERHAMPTON WANDERERS ....

Nickname:	Wolves
Ground:	Molineux
Capacity:	32,050
Manager:	Nuno Espírito Santo
Last Season:	7th
Star Player:	Raúl Jiménez
Key Signing:	Patrick Cutrone (AC Milan)

VERDICT:
Last season is going to take some beating alongside Europa League commitments, but Wolves should be just as strong.

QUIZ ANSWERS

Page 18-19: Quiz of the Season

1. Five (Stuart Armstrong, Mohamed Elyounoussi, Angus Gunn, Jannik Vestergaard and Danny Ings)
2. Dušan Tadić
3. Leganés
4. Celta Vigo
5. Ryan Bertrand (vs Leicester)
6. One (FA Cup replay vs Derby)
7. Brighton and Crystal Palace
8. True (vs Newcastle, Watford and Man Utd)
9. Danny Ings
10. Tyreke Johnson
11. Nathan Redmond and Michael Obafemi
12. Pierre-Emile Højbjerg (vs Leicester and Man City)
13. Angus Gunn
14. Steven Davis and Manolo Gabbiadini
15. Three (vs Everton, Leicester and Derby)
16. Three (vs Arsenal and Huddersfield; Leicester and Everton; Tottenham and Brighton)
17. James Ward-Prowse (January and March)
18. Newcastle
19. Matt Targett (vs Bournemouth)
20. Five (Yan Valery, Tyreke Johnson, Kayne Ramsay, Callum Slattery and Marcus Barnes)

Page 39: Puzzles

Unlock the answer
HASENHÜTTL

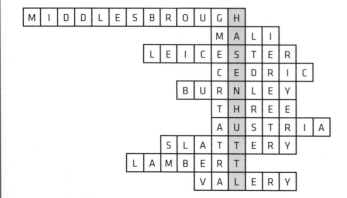

Name that Saint!

1. Jan Bednarek
2. Pierre-Emile Højbjerg
3. Charlie Austin
4. Ryan Bertrand
5. James Ward-Prowse
6. Yan Valery

Page 49: International Saints

1. Pierre-Emile Højbjerg
2. Jannik Vestergaard
3. Alex Mccarthy
4. Danny Ings
5. Nathan Redmond
6. Shane Long
7. Michael Obafemi
8. Moussa Djenepo
9. Mohamed Elyounoussi
10. Maya Yoshida
11. Cédric
12. Jan Bednarek
13. Stuart Armstrong
14. Josh Sims
15. James Ward-Prowse

WHICH RALPH ARE YOU?

CARING RALPH

COACHING RALPH

ADVENTUROUS RALPH

COMPETITIVE RALPH

CONSOLING RALPH

DEMANDING RALPH

FESTIVE RALPH

FOCUSED RALPH

FRIENDLY RALPH

FUN RALPH

FUNNY RALPH

HAPPY RALPH

HUNGRY RALPH

PASSIONATE RALPH

PROUD RALPH

SCARY RALPH

SHOWBOATING RALPH

WINNING RALPH